The Nature in Close-up Series

British Library Cataloguing in Publication Data

Free, John Brand
Life under Stones – (Nature in Close-up).
1. Invertebrates – Juvenile literature
I. Title II. Series
592 QL362

ISBN 0-7136-2121-4

Published by A & C Black (Publishers) Limited
35 Bedford Row, London WC1R 4JH

First published 1981

Filmset by Keyspools Ltd, Golborne, Lancs
Printed in Great Britain by Sackville Press Billericay Limited, Essex

Nature in Close-up

LIFE UNDER STONES

John B. Free

Adam & Charles Black · London

Contents

Introduction

If you lift a large stone, or a paving slab that has not been moved for some time, you will probably find several kinds of small animals living beneath it. There may be snails, slugs, worms, woodlice, earwigs, beetles, spiders and ants. They all live under stones for one or more of the following reasons.

1. Their bodies would dry out if exposed to sunlight. If they become too dry, these animals die. So slugs and other animals have to live in damp places – and it is nearly always damp under stones.

2. Stones give good protection against attacks from enemies. Watch the animals rush for safety when you lift the stone. Here you can see an earwig and its young.

3. Stones provide shelter during the day for animals which hunt at night, such as the Hunting Spider.

Some creatures, such as the woodlouse, live under stones for all these reasons.

Snails

If you find a snail, you will probably see only its head and foot. The rest of its body is coiled inside its shell.

The head has two pairs of horns. The smaller pair and the upper lip are for tasting and smelling; the tips of the larger pair carry the eyes, which do little more than tell the snail whether it is light or dark.

On the underside of the snail's head, there is a slime gland. This releases a silvery trail of slime along which the snail moves. If you look on the ground in the early morning, you may see the trails glistening in the sun.

Each snail has both male and female sex organs, but one snail has to mate with another before eggs are produced.
Soon after mating, the snail digs a hollow in the earth and lays its eggs there. When the young snails hatch they look just like their parents. They even have a tiny shell which gets bigger as they grow into adult snails.

▲ The snail glides along its slime trail by stretching and then contracting its foot.

The head of a snail showing its horns. These can be pulled in for protection. ▶

During the day, snails often shelter beneath stones, logs or flowerpots. They withdraw into their shells to avoid drying out. At night, they usually come out to feed, but if the weather is dry, they stay inactive.

Snails also withdraw into their shells during the winter. They close the mouth of the shell with a waterproof membrane – to keep moisture in, rather than keep it out.

Slugs

Slugs are similar to snails, although most species have lost all trace of a shell. But a few slugs do have a small shell near their tail; unlike most slugs these are meat-eaters and feed on earthworms.

Slugs have a variety of colours, and many have a pronounced frill around the foot. The Black Slug, one of the largest in Britain, has deep ridges running along its back.

Like snails, slugs are both male and female. Their eggs are laid in clumps.
Slugs are coated with a thick layer of slime to keep them moist. They leave trails of slime, which they may use to guide them back to their homes after feeding. Some slugs produce strings of slime that are thick and strong enough to suspend themselves on.

Because slugs have no shell, they dry out more quickly than snails and are more dependent on damp surroundings. They spend the day under stones, and only become active after rain and at night when it is cooler and damper.

◀ A slug lowers itself on a thick string of slime.

If disturbed, slugs protect themselves by shrinking into a small lump. In very cold or dry weather they tunnel deep into the soil.

Like snails, slugs have a rough tongue covered with hundreds of tiny horny teeth. They use their tongue to scrape up plant food, and they can cause serious damage in gardens.

▼ Like snails, slugs have two pairs of horns. The smaller pair are for tasting and smelling and the larger pair carry the eyes.

Earthworms

Earthworms make their burrows by eating their way through soil. If the soil becomes too cold, hot or dry, they tunnel deeper into the soil to where it is still moist. The skin of an earthworm must remain smooth and damp.

Earthworms emerge at night. Although they are blind, most of their body is sensitive to light, so enabling them to avoid it.

An earthworm disappears into its burrow. ▶

An earthworm's body is divided into segments. Each segment has a few bristles which allow it to grip the soil as it moves. If an earthworm is touched, it will quickly withdraw into its burrow and sink its bristles into the burrow wall. This is why birds have to pull hard to get an earthworm out of the soil.

The eggs of the earthworm are laid in a cocoon secreted from the band, or 'saddle', around its body.

Earthworms are very useful to farmers and gardeners because their burrows help air and water to circulate through the soil. They also help to increase the goodness of the soil by eating and digesting decaying matter.

The 'saddle' of the earthworm is the lighter patch around the middle of its body. ▶

Centipedes

Centipedes have slender, flat bodies divided into about 15 segments. Each segment has one pair of legs. The back pair is longer than the rest and probably bears senses of touch and smell although most of the sensory organs are at the head end. During the day, centipedes hide under stones. They make sure they are well hidden by placing their bodies in contact with their surroundings. In cold and dry conditions they burrow deep into the soil.

At night, centipedes hunt for food. They move very quickly seizing small animals with powerful claws at the front of their head. They then inject their prey with poison.

Millipedes

The bodies of millipedes are also divided into strips, or segments. Each segment has two pairs of legs. But millipedes are slow-moving; when they walk, their whitish legs appear to ripple in 'waves'.

Unlike centipedes, millipedes feed on plant material, mostly dead leaves or fungi. Like earthworms their feeding habits help to enrich the soil.

Some millipedes curl up into a flattish coil when disturbed. They are then too wide for the mouths of most of their enemies.

Millipedes lay their eggs in the soil, or under stones or bark. Their young look like small adults, except that they have fewer legs. They have to change their skins several times before they are mature.

▼ A nest of young millipedes.

Woodlice

Woodlice are always found in moist dark places. Their bodies are encased in broad, overlapping plates, but these don't prevent them from drying out. They feed at night, mostly on decaying vegetable matter.

Some woodlice (Pill Lice) curl up into a ball if they are alarmed. Their thick body plates protect them against attack from their smaller enemies.

All woodlice have many pairs of jointed legs; like centipedes, the back pair probably bears senses of touch and smell.

The female woodlouse has a 'brood pouch' on the underside of her body. This is for carrying her eggs. After hatching, the young woodlice stay in the pouch for a few days. They look like small adults, except that they are very pale.

▼ A young woodlouse.

Earwigs

Earwigs hide away from the light during the day. At night, they seek a variety of foods, including living and decaying plant material and small insects and mites.

Earwigs mate and breed under stones. You can tell the difference between male and female earwigs by the shape of their pincers; the male's pincers are more strongly curved than the female's.

In early spring, the female drives away her mate and lays her eggs in the soil. She stays with her eggs, frequently licking and turning them over to keep them free of mould. If disturbed, she arches her tail and pincers over her body, ready to defend her brood.

Young earwigs are white when they hatch, and lack the wings and wing cases of the adult. They stay with their mother for several weeks after they hatch while she feeds and cares for them.

Gradually, the young earwigs begin to look for food and learn to defend themselves.

Beetles

Dark brown and black beetles of many shapes and sizes live under stones. Beetle larvae can also be found. The adults hide during the day and hunt and feed at night.

When exposed to the light, many ground beetles scuttle away or attempt to take flight. If the Coach-horse Beetle is disturbed, it rears up, raises its tail like an earwig and opens its jaws wide to defend itself.

Spiders

A variety of spiders live under stones. Some, such as the Wolf Spider, can look quite fierce. The spiders lie in wait for insects, woodlice and smaller spiders, and then pounce on them. They catch their victims with their front legs and inject them with poison from their poison fangs.

All spiders produce silk, and most use it to make webs. Spiders also spin their silk into cocoons to hold their eggs. Some spiders attach these cocoons to the undersides of stones.

Wolf Spiders carry their cocoons beneath their bodies. After hatching, the young spiders stay on their mother's back for a few days.

◀ Spider's eggs in a silk cocoon.

▼ The hunting spider lies in wait for its prey.

Ants

A large flat stone often forms the roof of an ant nest. Beneath it, tunnels and chambers branch out in all directions.

Ants are social insects and live together in colonies. Each colony has a queen and hundreds of workers. Winged males are born in summer.

The workers do all the jobs in the nest, including caring for the queen and her young, building and maintaining the tunnels, looking for food (mainly small insects) and defending the colony.

Worker ants look after the larvae ▶
and pupae.

▼ Inside an ant nest. The ants stay in the same nest for at least a year.

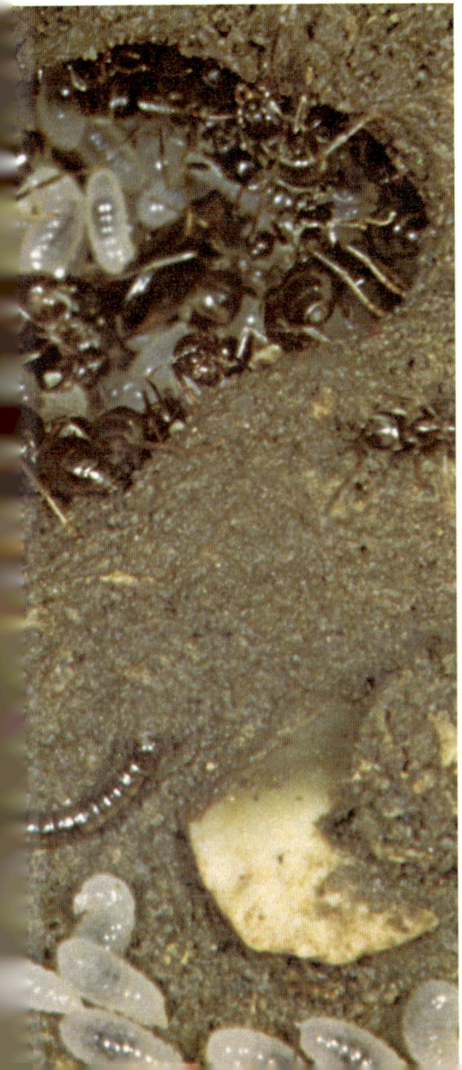

The larvae and pupae can often be seen in the chambers immediately beneath the stone. The workers move the young about to make sure they are in the best places in the nest.

Ant larvae look like legless colourless grubs. The pale, paper-like cocoons contain the pupae. The large cocoons contain the pupae of the young queens.

If the nest is disturbed, the workers seize the larvae and pupae and carry them in their jaws to a safe place deep down in the soil.

When the weather starts to get cold or dry, the ants withdraw into the depths of the nest. They remain inactive until the warm spring sunshine wakes them up. Then they come out to look for food.

The queens are much larger than the workers and they have wings. On a sunny day in summer, they fly away from the nest to start a nest of their own.

▼ Queen ants have wings and are much larger than the other ants. They are looked after by the workers and hardly ever leave the nest.

Index